Mantled
for
Manifestation

Mantled for Manifestation

"A 21 DAY GUIDE FOR PRAYER & FASTING"

Roneshia Anderson

Unless otherwise noted, all scripture quotations are taken from the King James Version of the Bible.

Scriptures taken from the Holy Bible, New International Version®, NIV®. Copyright © 1973, 1978, 1984, 2011 by Biblica, Inc.™ Used by permission of Zondervan. All rights reserved worldwide. www.zondervan.com The "NIV" and "New International Version" are trademarks registered in the United States Patent and Trademark Office by Biblica, Inc.™

Scripture taken from the Amplified Bible, Copyright © 1954, 1958, 1962, 1964, 1965, 1987 by The Lockman Foundation. Used by permission.

ISBN: 1724231421
ISBN-13: 9781724231420

To Holy Spirit,
You are the perfect inspiration
&
To my mom, Sarah,
who I watched fast many days,
while still cooking for her family.

FOREWORD

W*ere not our hearts burning within us?* These were the words spoken by the disciples after they met Jesus along the road to Emmaus. It was my response as well upon reading this Holy Spirit breathed and inspired book. I've been walking with the Lord for a long time and although this is a book of prayer and fasting, it speaks to the depths of hearts and causes the true believer to examine themselves.

Jesus called out His disciples for their weakness of faith. Roneshia is challenging each of us to couple the Word of God with prayer and fasting so that we can be strong in our faith and show God's power and allow His kingdom to be made manifest through us on the earth.

Listen, it is imperative that we cultivate lifestyles of prayer and fasting. Roneshia profoundly, yet simply, teaches us in this book what this looks like. You want to be counted by God among His sheep, so you have a decision to make—either you press in and worship Him in spirit and in truth (prayer & fasting is a way of life, not just isolated moments) or keep yielding to carnality and miss out on knowing who He is.

The time is now, prepare your hearts and turn down your plates so you too can be *Mantled for Manifestation!*

Candace A. Jones
Author, *For Such A Time As This*

CONTENTS

Week Three: MANTLED FOR MANIFESTATION

INTRODUCTION

Jesus said to them, "My food is to do the will of Him who sent Me and to completely finish His work
❧ John 4:34, NIV☙

Mantled for Manifestation began as a 21 day fast initiated by Holy Spirit. He told me that we were coming out with receipts, but I didn't know a book would be one of them. The Bible does speak of God's ways and thoughts being higher than ours (Isaiah 55:9). I was surprised to have 21 ladies agree to seek the Lord with me. We bombarded the heavens with prayer and fasting for 21-25 days, because Holy Spirit decided to extend our fast. Not only did we refrain from food, but we also pulled back from social media. The internet is a great tool, and I often wonder how fast the gospel would have spread if our favorite Bible characters had access to the world wide web.

We are living in the age of social media. There's Instagram, Facebook, Twitter, SnapChat, YouTube, and the list goes on and on. Manifestation appears to be one of the hot topics in my news feed. I see a lot of people talking about promises coming to pass, but I wonder how many are prepared to handle everything that follows. When most think about manifestation, they're just focused on receiving what they have been praying for. Many don't ponder the spiritual warfare, persecution, separation of family and friends, etc., that could be attached to that promise. What about the manifestation of Biblical prophecy--the scary stuff? You know, the things that you try to bind and rebuke, not realizing that everything can't be prayed away.

I believe that many won't see the wonderful manifestations they are proclaiming, because they haven't prepared for it. God is gracious and merciful, but He isn't going to release much to the unprepared. This release is coming to those who are integral, trustworthy, humble, and obedient! It's coming to those who seek the heart and mind of God, not just His hand (provision). Tell me this, how does it benefit you to talk about what God is doing if you neglect to prepare for it? Why brag about hearing God if you aren't going to obey Him? If God has not mantled you for these manifestations, you will either miss or mishandle the release. A mishandled harvest leads to a missing harvest, because if you don't prepare for it; you'll lose it.

If you follow me on Facebook, you know that I tend

to write a lot. One of the challenges with this book was having to compact loads of information. I wanted this guide to be simple enough that the "unchurched" could follow it, but so powerful that an experienced faster receives renewal from it. Asking God to mantle you for manifestation is equivalent to asking Him to clothe you for what's coming. Preparation is the garment of any good soldier! My prayer is that this book thrusts you into a lifestyle of prayer and fasting. I pray that you receive a fresh hunger and thirst for the Word and will of God. It's time to begin your process of being mantled!

A Lethal Combination

How be it this kind goeth not out but by prayer and fasting
❧ Matthew 17:21 ❧

Prayer and fasting is great, but combining the two makes you a force to be reckoned with. We love grabbing combos at our favorite fast food restaurants, but how often do you order this combination? Please understand that certain manifestations will never hit your life unless you turn your plate down and cry out to God. Let's briefly talk about prayer and fasting.

Prayer is simply communication between you and God. A common mistake made in prayer is that a lot of times we go in doing all the talking. How would you like it if you were conversing with someone who never allowed you to speak? You would ignore their next phone call or walk the opposite way if you saw them in a store. Thank goodness God is not like man. He continues to answer, but you need to allow Him to speak.

It's interesting how we sometimes make the things of God more difficult than they really are. One of my biggest breakthroughs in prayer happened many years ago. Prayer became so much easier when I learned to have a conversation with God like He was sitting right in front of me. I received another level of breakthrough by being transparent in prayer. See, I would go to God trying to mask hurts as if everything was ok. I must've forgotten that He knows all so there was no need to try and hide. Abba is a good Father, who has your best interest at heart, and He longs to spend time with you.

Before we discuss what fasting is, let's talk about what it is not. Fasting is not a tool used to manipulate God. You should never fast in hopes to twist God's arm on a matter. We can't manipulate God! You should never pray and fast for the downfall of another individual—that's witchcraft. Remember that we wrestle not against flesh and blood but against powers and principalities (Eph. 6:12).

Fasting is when you abstain from eating and drinking, for a period, to seek God. Most of us don't eat as healthy as we should, so I recommend drinking water to flush toxins out of your body while fasting. If Holy Spirit leads you to fast for several days with no food or water, I believe that He will grace you for it. I understand that everyone does not operate at the same level of faith, so you may not fast for 21 days at first. You may not fast for a full 24 hours the first time, but God honors pure sacrifices.

I've heard many speak about fasting from Facebook, sweets, or meats, but I would consider those consecrations. You should live a life of consecration, but there are times you need to turn your plate down completely. A lot of times people abstain from a certain food, but they overindulge in another, which defeats the purpose. Please know that I'm not a medical doctor, and I do not want a lawsuit, so I'm unable to recommend specific fasts to you. I have done everything from 24, 48, and 72 hour fasts to 7 days with no food. I have also fasted for 21 days, and I've done a 40-day consecration from sweets. I normally don't tell others when I'm on a fast unless it's a corporate one. I did not share my history to brag about what I've done but to bring credibility to the birthing of this book. I'm no expert, but I have enough experience to help those who struggle in this area. I encourage you to research the diverse types of fasts and allow Holy Spirit to direct you on which one to do.

Pair your favorite journal with this guide and document your thoughts for each day. The space provided may not be enough if you enjoy writing.

Week 1:

God, Cleanse Me

Day 1

The Man in the Mirror

Have mercy upon me, O God, according unto the multitude of Thy tender mercies blot out my transgressions.
Psalms 51:1

We often see posts or hear sermons that talk about haters. Although they do exist, I think we should evaluate ourselves more. It seems as if some of us believe God's blessings are for us but not our haters. At the end of the day, all our righteousness are as filthy rags (Isaiah 64:6). We all need the grace and mercy of God!

Ask God to show you yourself today. Ask Him to expose everything in you that is not pleasing in His sight. You can be your worst enemy at times, so don't fight when He exposes things you don't want to see. We all fall short, time after time, and can't make it without the help of God. He wants you to rely on Him! You can trust Him with the ugliest parts of your inner being. It's time to be real with yourself and your Savior! Allow Him to be your safe place and know that you don't have to hide anymore!

Prayer

Holy Spirit, I am a mess. Please reveal everything in me that is not like You. (Insert what you need help with.) I know that You're already aware of these things, but I am asking for Your help. Help me to understand that my sins don't change the love You have for me. I know that You desire my deliverance more than I want it. Thank You for allowing me to see what I need to change. I love You Holy Spirit!

Document Your Thoughts

Day 2

WASH ME

Wash me thoroughly from mine iniquity and cleanse me from my sin. For I acknowledge my transgressions: and my sin is ever before me

☙ Psalms 51:2-3 ❧

Now that you have acknowledged your sins, you need washing. There is a special healing and anointing associated with water. One misunderstanding some have is thinking they must clean themselves up before coming to God. Dear hearts, if you had the ability to save yourself, you wouldn't need God.

The best way for spiritual cleansing is drenching yourself in God's Word. If the King James Version is difficult for you to read, download the Bible app. Use this app to compare different versions of the Bible, until you find the version you want to buy. If needed, you can even Google scriptures that relate to your struggle.

Don't make the mistake of comparing your study time to someone else's. Everyone is not on the same level, and the spirit of comparison desires to cripple you. Focus on developing and maintaining your relationship with God. Pursue His Word and you'll grow in ways that you cannot imagine.

Prayer

Holy Spirit, I repent for my sins. Please forgive me and wash me with Your Word. Give me an unquenchable hunger and thirst for You. Feed me until I want some more! Holy Spirit, I need You to open the scriptures up to me. Keep me from feeling overwhelmed when I'm trying to study. I crave You more than I want food. I long for Your Word more than my flesh desires to sin. Thank You for cleansing me. I love You!

Document Your Thoughts

Day 3

CLEAN HANDS & PURE HEARTS

Who shall ascend into the hill of the LORD? Or who shall stand in His holy place? He that hath clean hands, and a pure heart; who hath not lifted up his soul unto vanity, nor sworn deceitfully.

❧ Psalms 24:3-4 ☙

God is looking for integral people to handle His business. It's disheartening that many don't want anything to do with the church these days because they've seen so much mess in ministry. I know it appears as if some are getting away with their foolishness, but don't be distracted by the chaos. The tables are turning! God's grace sometimes allows the anointing to fall on leaders during a message, for the sake of the congregation, but He is tired of those living double lives.

This harvest is coming to those who have clean hands and pure hearts. The release many are waiting on is for those who live just as holy in private as they do in public. Will you be perfect? No, but I think it's possible for us to live a lot closer to perfection than we currently do. It helps to just slow down and take things one day at a time.

Prayer

I desire to stand in Your Holy place Jesus. I want to become one with You. Please help me to keep my hands clean and my heart pure. Help me not to compromise my morals for money. Disrupt every ungodly connection in my life. Sever the ties no matter how bad it hurts me. Connect me with like-minded people who will hold me accountable. Keep me from developing hidden motives and agendas. Help me from becoming bitter towards those who have done me wrong. Help me to remember that my first goal is for You to be pleased with everything I say and do. I love You!

Document Your Thoughts

Day 4

Stay with Me

Cast me not away from Thy presence; and take not Thy Holy Spirit from me.

Psalms 51:11

If I were to take a poll of the top 10 favorite Bible characters, more than likely, David would be on everybody's list. Honestly, he would be in the top five! I absolutely adore David, but he did some jacked up stuff. David committed adultery, got the woman pregnant, and then had her husband killed.

This scripture is a song David wrote after being confronted by the Prophet Nathan. I love the fact that David didn't deny his sin. Although he was guilty, David still asked God not to leave him. He desired communion with God over the lust of his flesh. I sometimes tell Holy Spirit that if He leaves me, I will stalk Him. I know it sounds crazy, but you'd have to understand our relationship. I need Him! What I don't want you to do is drown in guilt and condemnation, because you are not what you've done! God called David a man after His own heart, and He can still use you, if you're willing.

Prayer

Holy Spirit, I repent for grieving You. I know that I don't always do what's right, but I can't live without Your presence! I need You more than I needed my last breath! I need You even more than I need my next breath! I don't want to live a day without You, and I have no life apart from You. I know we don't live by feeling, but I long to feel Your presence. Please, stay with me! I love You.

Document Your Thoughts

Day 5

OFFENSE BE GONE

Ye have heard that it hath been said, Thou shalt love thy neighbor, and hate thine enemy. But I say unto you, love your enemies, bless them that curse you, do good to them that hate you, and pray for them which despitefully use you, and persecute you;

Matthew 5:43-44

It's time to release people who have offended you. I know it's easier said than done, but you must let it go. It hurts, and you have the right to be upset, but you deserve to be free. Forgiveness is more for you than it is for the one who offended you. You also need to learn how to accept the apologies you'll never get. One of the worst things you can do is wait for a person to say, "I'm sorry," before you forgive them. It's best to practice forgiving the moment you are offended. Protect your peace, forgive people, and release them to God. Practice speaking the blessing of the Lord over those who want you dead. I want you to get a sheet of paper and a pen. Make a list of people that you need to forgive and pray for them.

Prayer

Holy Spirit, help me to release all those who have offended me. What they did hurt, and I cannot do this in my own strength. Your Word says that Your strength is made perfect in my weakness, and I believe Your Word! I'm fully relying on You to get me through this. I release and forgive (Insert name here), and I pray the blessing of the Lord over them. I know that this may not happen overnight but give me a pure heart towards them. I decree that it is so, in Jesus' name, Amen!

> **Do this as many days as needed until it becomes genuine.*

Document Your Thoughts

Day 6

DIG DEEPER

Jesus said to them, "My food is to do the will of Him who sent Me and to completely finish His work
❧ Mark 11:25-26 ☙

Yesterday we dealt with offense, and I know it wasn't an easy task. Honestly, today is going to be more difficult for you. It's time to release people you won't acknowledge. Let me explain what I mean. You need to release those who've hurt you, although you don't want to admit it's affecting you. They could be parents who were absent, even if they were present, or the person who molested you as a child. Perhaps it's a convict who killed your relative, or an ex who abused you. Some of you are even holding grudges against people who are deceased. How would you feel knowing that the person you're upset with repented and made it into Heaven, but you ended up in Hell, because you couldn't release what they did to you?

You've done all you could to suppress the painful memories. You may have even used men, women, or drugs to cope. If anyone tried to bring up the topic, you quickly changed the subject. It's time to deal with these issues head on because unforgiveness breeds bitter hearts. Bitterness then causes you to bleed on others who had nothing to do with your pain. Many relationships have suffered and ended because of this. You must dig deep, release what you've suppressed, and begin your healing process. For some, the altar alone works, but others may need counseling after leaving the altar. I believe in both!

Prayer

Holy Spirit, help me to confront the hard things. I know that I've been acting as if I'm over what happened to me, but I'm not. Deep down it really does bother me, and I don't want to live a life of bitterness. I am ready to be free from this hurt. I release and forgive (insert name here), and I pray the blessing of the Lord over them. I release (insert deceased name here), and the painful memories they left me with. I also release and forgive myself! I am not responsible for what others did to me. I will no longer be bound by my past. I am free in Christ, in Jesus' name, Amen!

Document Your Thoughts

Day 7

INVITE ABBA IN

May He grant you out of the riches of His glory, to be strengthened and spiritually energized with power through His Spirit in your inner self, [indwelling your innermost being and personality], so that Christ may dwell in your hearts through your faith. And may you having been [deeply] rooted and [securely] grounded in love, be fully capable of comprehending with all the saints (God's people) the width and length and height and depth of His love [fully experiencing that amazing, endless love]; and [that you may come] to know, [practically, through personal experience] the love of Christ which far surpasses [mere] knowledge [without experience], that you may be filled up [throughout your being] to all the fullness of God [so that you may have the richest experience of God's presence in your lives, completely filled and flooded with God Himself].

Ephesians 3:16-19, AMP

Abba is the perfect Father, and you should let Him love you! Yes, I know that He loves everyone, but don't forget that love is an action word. God desires to show you how much He loves you. Whether we like to admit it or not, the experiences we've had with our natural parents can change our perception of God. You may have had parents who only made broken promises, so you don't fully trust God. You've always been let down, used, or manipulated by every authority figure you've had, so why should you view God any different? I want to share a story that will help you understand what I mean.

My dad died when I was 12, and I believe that I've been pushing people away ever since. I've always been very mature for my age; like most girls I guess. When my dad got sick, my mom would just say, "Pray, because God hears children's prayers." I thought my dad was going to be healed, because I kept praying. I awaited the manifestation of his healing each day. I watched him die for months, but my faith never wavered. I knew God heard my prayers! No matter how bad the situation got, my faith was unshakeable. If only I had that level of faith today! Pain ravished me when my dad died, so I got mad at God and developed a defense mechanism. I felt like my mom should have told me that death was a possibility, because I thought I was mature enough to handle it. I imagined that building walls would protect me from being hurt again.

I didn't stay mad at God for long because I knew better. I wouldn't let anyone get close to me after that. If someone managed to get too close, I pushed them away. My dad left me, so in the back of my mind, anyone who got close to me would just end up leaving, one way or another. Approximately ten years ago, Holy Spirit arrested me in prayer. He let me know that I was treating Him just like a human being. When He tried to get too close, I'd push Him away as well. I also didn't feel worthy to be loved by God. When He told me that I had walls up against Him, I wept sore!

Evaluate your life to see if there are any areas you've blocked God from. We often trust Him in one area but not another. You trust Him with your finances, but not your love life. You trust Him with your health, but not your money. You trust Him to heal everyone else, but you accept every negative report the doctor gives you. Don't you think it's time to grant Him full access?

Prayer

Abba, I'm sorry for treating You like man. I admit that I don't know how to properly love or be loved by You. I need You to teach me. Repair my distorted vision of You so that I'm able to see clearly. You are my Heavenly Father who only wants what's best for me. You loved me so much that you sent Your son Jesus to die for me. You knew the mistakes I would make before my conception, yet You didn't cancel my appointment with destiny. I know that You desire a close relationship with me. In faith, I speak to the walls I've built and command them to come down now! Drench me in Your love and clothe me with Your affirmation! It is done now in the name that is above every name! Thanks Jesus!

Document Your Thoughts

Week 2:

God, Fill Me Again

Day 8

Increase My Capacity for You

Then the disciples of John [the Baptist] came to Jesus, asking, "Why do we and the Pharisees often fast [as a religious exercise], but your disciples do not fast?' And Jesus replied to them, "Can the guests of the bridegroom mourn while the bridegroom is with them? The days will come when the bridegroom is taken away from them, and then they will fast. But no one puts a piece of unshrunk (new) cloth on an old garment; for the patch pulls away from the garment, and a worse tear results. Nor is new wine put into old wineskins [that have lost their elasticity]; otherwise the wineskins burst, and the [fermenting] wine spills and the wineskins are ruined. But new wine is put into fresh wineskins, so both are preserved.

❧ Matthew 9:14-17, AMP ❧

Let's discuss the importance of new wineskin. When making wine in Israel, they would store it in the skin of an animal, normally a goat. The animal's skin would be made into a bag, and the new wine would be poured in. As the wine fermented, the new animal skin would stretch and harden to accommodate what it was carrying. I could run right there! If they tried using old wineskins to hold new wine, the old skins would burst due to the fermentation process of the new wine. They'd be left with good wine that was wasted, because it was placed in an old vessel that was unable to preserve it. Processing is vital!

Do you see why self-evaluation is needed? How are you going to hold what God releases without preparation? You don't want to be another old vessel, living a raggedy life, while trying to carry the things of God. This is an issue in the body of Christ. There are too many people trying to carry fresh word, revelations, and gifts while neglecting the process. You don't want to waste anything God entrusts you with. Ask Holy Spirit to increase your capacity for Him!

Prayer

Holy Spirit, I need You to make me over. Cover me with new skin in the Spirit, because I can't afford to waste what You are releasing to me. Help me to stretch so that I can hold all that You desire to place on the inside. Allow my skin to harden so that I can make it through the persecution and processing I will face in the coming days. I even command my organs, cells, and tissues to come into alignment with the blood, will, Word, and name of Jesus Christ! Help me to remain integral as my capacity increases for You. I don't ever want to think I know it all, so help me to forever be a student of Your Word! Stretch and prepare me to carry and maintain the revelation

You've placed on the inside. I can't afford to waste Your wine, in Jesus' name, Amen!

Document Your Thoughts

Day 9

Fill Me Again

And I say unto you, Ask, and it shall be given you; seek, and ye shall find; knock, and it shall be opened unto you. For everyone that asketh receiveth; and he that seeketh findeth; and to him that knocketh it shall be opened. If a son shall ask bread of any of you that is a father, will he give him a stone? Or if he ask a fish, will he for a fish give him a serpent? Or if he shall ask an egg, will he offer him a scorpion? If ye then, being evil, know how to give good gifts unto your children: how much more shall your heavenly Father give the Holy Spirit to them that ask Him?

Luke 11:9-13

Have you ever heard the phrase, "You should never be satisfied with yesterday's anointing"? It's a true statement. We sometimes get stuck in what God has done, but He's so much bigger than His last great move. I think many focus on the initial infilling of Holy Spirit but that's it. You should consistently ask Holy Spirit to fill you all over again. Ask Him to baptize you with His Spirit. In the natural, you work on keeping healthy relationships, and you should do the same with Holy Spirit. Let Him know that you long to keep your relationship fresh! I tend to hear people say a man or woman is the best thing that has ever happened to them. Clearly, they haven't had a relationship with Holy Spirit yet.

Prayer

Holy Spirit, anoint me afresh! Fill and baptize me with Your Spirit all over again. It is in You that I live, move, and have my very being. Anoint me with fresh fire! I want to feel the Glory of God! Consume my mind and my members. Burn out everything in me that is not like You. Help me to always remain aware of Your presence. If I ever begin to neglect You, check me quickly! My relationship with You is more important than any relationship I have in the natural. I love You Holy Spirit!

Document Your Thoughts

Day 10

Renew My Mind

I beseech you therefore, brethren, by the mercies of God, that ye present your bodies a living sacrifice, holy, acceptable unto God, which is your reasonable service. And be not conformed to this world: but be ye transformed by the renewing of your mind, that ye may prove what is that good, and acceptable, and perfect, will of God.

❧ Romans 12:1-2 ☙

Mental warfare is real, and one of the greatest battles that you'll ever face will be in your mind. You may have already experienced times when you had to fight for your sanity. Ask God to renew your mind through His Word daily. Transformation is impossible without a renewed mind. You will not be able to keep the release that's coming if you are mentally unstable. Guard you ear and eye gates! Many of you don't understand how the enemy uses media and arts/entertainment to invade your mind.

You can't watch every television show, and you can't listen to every song on the radio. That includes secular and Christian music, no matter how popular it might be. Let me help you by taking it a step further--You can't answer every phone call, and you don't need to open every text message. Protect your mind, and don't apologize for doing so!

Prayer

Holy Spirit, give me the mind of Christ. Renew my mind daily so that my thoughts and actions remain sober. Help me not to conform to the world's standards, even if the majority agrees. Prepare my mind for what's about to manifest. I cast down every imagination and high thing that's trying to exalt itself against the knowledge of God! I bring into captivity every thought to the obedience of Christ! Holy Spirit, you are the best Psychologist that I could ever have! Teach me how to protect my mind! I thank You in advance for a supernatural metamorphosis as it relates to my thought life. It's in Jesus' name that I pray, Amen!

Document Your Thoughts

Day 11

Holy Spirit, Reveal Yourself

And I will ask the Father, and He will give you another Helper (Comforter, Advocate, Intercessor—Counselor, Strengthener, Standby), to be with you forever—the Spirit of Truth, whom the world cannot receive [and take to its heart] because it does not see Him or know Him, but you know Him because He (the Holy Spirit) remains with you continually and will be in you. I will not leave you as orphans [comfortless, bereaved, and helpless]; I will come [back] to you.

John 14:16-18, AMP

It seems as if Holy Spirit is sometimes the forgotten member of the Godhead. Even some who are Spirit filled tend to neglect Him at times. Do you really understand that the same Spirit who raised Jesus from the dead lives on the inside of you? Ask Him to reveal Himself! There is nothing wrong with being deep in God, because His depth is immeasurable. I converse with Holy Spirit daily, and I refuse to do life without Him. His power is so real! I recommend that you read, *Good Morning, Holy Spirit* by Benny Hinn, if you haven't already. He does an excellent job at describing how tangible Holy Spirit really is. If you have not received the infilling of Holy Spirit yet, read Acts chapters 1 & 2. This filling doesn't require you tarrying at an altar. You can receive Him right now by faith. Although there is more to being filled than speaking in tongues, I do believe this is the first sign.

Prayer—Desiring to be Filled with Holy Spirit

Father God in the precious name of Jesus, I repent for all my sins. Please forgive me for all unrighteousness. Holy Spirit, I believe You came down on the day of Pentecost and never left. You're the perfect Gift from Heaven, and I'm ready to receive You. I'm asking in faith for You to fill every part of my being. Fill me until I speak in a heavenly language. Fill me until I'm walking in power and demonstration. Fill me until miracles, signs, and wonders are wrought through my hands. I thank You in advance for filling me with Your Spirit.

❧

> *Some of you may begin to speak in tongues, by faith, at once. If you don't, just continue to ask and thank Him in advance.*

Prayer—For the Spirit-filled Ones

Holy Spirit, I want You to reveal Yourself to me. I already know You as God the Spirit and (Insert who He is to you), but I don't want to put You in a box. There's so much depth to You that I haven't seen, and I long for the supernatural. I want as much of You as I can handle on this side of Heaven. Help me to stop expecting You to speak the same way every time. I am open for however You wish to speak to me. I command my five senses to stand at attention as it relates to Your voice. Reveal Yourself!

Day 12

FAITH IT

Cast not away therefore your confidence, which hath great recompense of reward. For ye have need of patience; that, after ye have done the will of God, ye might receive the promise. For yet a little while, and he that shall come will come, and will not tarry. Now the just shall live by faith: but if any man draw back, my soul shall have no pleasure in him.

❧ Hebrews 10:35-38 ☙

Now faith is the substance of things hoped for, the evidence of things not seen.

❧ Hebrews 11:1 ☙

But without faith it is impossible to please Him: for he that cometh to God must believe that He is, and that He is a rewarder of them that diligently seek Him.

❧ Hebrews 11:6 ☙

Faith is essential when asking God to mantle you for manifestation. Many people don't think they have enough faith, but I beg to differ. You have more faith than you realize; just exercise it. The fact that you bought this book means that you have faith. Fasting is an act of faith. Prayer is an act of faith. Believing in Jesus requires faith. You can't obtain salvation without faith. If you are one of the ones who's been talking about manifestation, your speech is an act of faith. This next great move of God will be led by groups of men and women who are operating in unshakeable faith.

Instead of beating yourself up about not having enough faith, try exercising the amount you do have. Start by decreeing something that you're believing God for. The Bible talks about you decreeing a thing and it being established (Job 22:28). Speak it until it manifests, then believe God for something bigger. Regardless of what the situation looks like in the natural, try not to let your faith waiver. Picture faith as a skinny man that lifts weights in the gym each day. He starts off slim, but the more he exercises, the bigger he gets. Exercise your faith and watch it grow! Even when you can't explain it, faith it!

Prayer

Holy Spirit, help me to exercise my faith. There is so much I'm believing You for and faith is a necessity. I don't want to get stuck on what I see in the natural. I need blind faith. I must believe You even when I don't see a way out. I don't know what's going to happen in this world, but Your Word says the just live by faith. While the Bible continues to fulfill itself, I'm going to need strong faith to stand. You're the God who kept the children of Israel in the wilderness! You're the God who made water stand at attention for Your people! You're the same God who answered Elijah by fire on Mt. Carmel, and You sent provision to a widow who was preparing to die! You're the God who raised the dead and fed a party of more than 5,000 with two fish and five loaves of bread! I just believe that if You did it before; You can do it again!

Document Your Thoughts

Day 13

A Fresh Yes

And He [Jesus] went a little farther, and fell on his face, and prayed, saying, O my Father, if it be possible, let this cup pass from me: nevertheless, not as I will, but as thou wilt.

Matthew 26:39

If you desire to be mantled, submitting to God's perfect will is key. You must put yourself on the altar every single day. Crucifying your flesh will also teach you spiritual discipline. You cannot be a true disciple of Christ if you're undisciplined. Jesus is our example in all things, but even He had a moment in the garden. He asked Abba to get Him out of His assignment, if it was possible, but then Jesus put His feelings aside and submitted to God's will. He had a moment but moved on. It's ok for you to have moments as well. Kick, cry, scream, do whatever is necessary, but after your tantrum, wipe the tears and tell God, "YES!" Once you practice submission to God; you'll quickly find out that there will always be another YES that He requires of you. You will move out of your comfort zone!

<u>Prayer</u>

Holy Spirit, help me submit to Your will, Your way. Honestly, I'm afraid but I can't afford to disobey You. I need to follow Your instructions, and I vow to do what you say, even when I'm scared. I know that the safest place is in Your will! Teach me how to put myself on the altar daily and present my body as a living sacrifice. Holy Spirit, I realize that You are perfect Help, and I know You'll be with me every step of the way. Today I say YES to doing things Your way!

Document Your Thoughts

Day 14

Focus

For I reckon that the sufferings of this present time are not worthy to be compared with the glory which shall be revealed in us.
Romans 8:18

I want you to use this day to reflect. The first thirteen days were intense, and I don't want you to get overwhelmed. Review and pray over the areas that were most difficult for you. Life has a way of hitting you so hard that victory can seem unattainable. Be encouraged because glory is coming! That's another reason the first seven days are extremely important. It's dangerous to call on the glory of God, when you aren't living a clean life, because the glory can kill you. Don't play with it! I know that you've suffered, but God is preparing you to be revealed. I want to pray over you now.

I bind every tormenting spirit in your mind! I bind every demon that has been telling you that you're wasting time trying to live right! I bind every spirit of fear that keeps telling you that you're going to die prematurely! I bind every demonic force that wants to make you think the generational curses in your family will never break! Every spirit that is saying you'll die in poverty, abuse, lack, disease, etc.--I throw the blood of Jesus on them at once! May God release His strong angels to prevail against every demon that has been torturing you! I believe that even hell can sense the move of God that's coming, and they are trying to do everything in their power to keep many of you distracted and stuck. Don't fall for hell's bait! You are more than a conqueror through Christ Jesus! I decree that you'll never be the same after reading this book, in Jesus' name, Amen!

Document Your Thoughts

Week 3:

Mantled for Manifestation

Day 15

TRUST ME

But just as we have been approved by God to be entrusted with the gospel [that tells the good news of salvation through faith in Christ], so we speak, not as [if we were trying] to please people [to gain power and popularity], but to please God who examines our hearts [expecting our best].

1 Thessalonians 2:4

Being chosen by God is an honor that is sometimes taken for granted. Please don't walk around thinking you're irreplaceable. God wants to use you, but if you refuse, He can and will find someone else. If you're a carrier of the gospel and gifts of God, you should be walking in humility, not arrogance. The days of the raggedy reigning is over, and the righteous remnant is rising again. God is looking for those He can trust with His next move. He wants people who'll do His will without stealing His Glory. He needs those who are willing to give up all they have known just to follow Him.

Prayer

Holy Spirit, please trust me with Your Word and gifts. Help me to always be an integral carrier of the gospel of Jesus Christ. I don't want to steal Your glory because it's not about me. Help me to speak what You say even when the message isn't a popular one. Fame is not my goal, and I want to remain humble on any platform you provide. I'm not sure why You choose me for this assignment, but I promise not to take You or it for granted. Lord, You can trust me.

Document Your Thoughts

Day 16

Mantle Me

I will greatly rejoice in the Lord, my soul shall be joyful in my God; for he hath clothed me with the garments of salvation, he hath covered me with the robe of righteousness, as a bridegroom decketh himself with ornaments, and as a bride adorneth herself with her jewels. For as the earth bringeth forth her bud, and as the garden causeth the things that are sown in it to spring forth; so the Lord God will cause righteousness and praise to spring forth before all the nations.

❧ Isaiah 61:10-11 ❧

Asking God to mantle you for manifestation is equivalent to saying, "Lord, prepare me!" When most think of manifestation they focus on answered prayers, miracles, promotions, etc. I wonder how many think about all sides of manifestation. What about the Bible fulfilling itself concerning wars and rumors of wars? What about the persecution that comes along with manifestation or just being a Christian? What about the mocking and scourging from people who'll think you're crazy for having faith in God? What are you going to do when it seems as if the world is fighting to pull Jesus out of everything? What would you do if execution for believing in Jesus became common in America?

Mantled for Manifestation is about being prepared for the good and the bad. It's interesting that people like to say, "I'm a soldier in the army of the Lord"! Let's not forget that many soldiers have given their lives for what they believe. Are you willing to physically die for Christ if you had to? I know that there are wonderful benefits that come along with being in the military. My dad is a deceased veteran, so I also know the painful side of the military. There are intense trainings and wars you must undergo and fight when you're a soldier. We need to be prepared for everything that is about to manifest—the good and the bad. Now do you see why exercising your faith in God is so important?

Prayer

Holy Spirit, I need You to clothe me for what's coming. I may not know everything that is about to happen, but I want to be as prepared as possible. Everything won't feel good, but I believe that it will all work for my good. I'm not sure what sacrifices You'll demand of me, but I'm asking for strength to stand. Clothe me in righteousness, integrity, honor, humility, and boldness. Help me to not fear men and their faces. Let my love for You be greater than the fear of man. Let my desire to please You be greater than my need for man's approval. I must obey, in Jesus' name, Amen.

Document Your Thoughts

Day 17

THY KINGDOM COME

Thy kingdom come. Thy will be done in earth, as it is in heaven.

☙ Matthew 6:10 ❧

Today you're going to focus on calling the power, fire, and glory of God from Heaven to earth. Pray that the Kingdom and will of God hits the earth like never before. Pray until your angels gain breakthrough in the Heavens and delivers your answers on the earth. Pray that men and women of God continue to yield to His will. Pray that the body of Christ rises and becomes the church that Jesus originally intended. Ask God to connect and reconnect men and women for His divine purpose. Ask Him to download kingdom principles, wisdom, and desires into you.

Prayer

Holy Spirit, I need to see Your power. I'm not satisfied with "church" as usual. I'm not satisfied with just hearing, reading, and watching videos about great revivals in history. You are the same God today that You were back then. I'm hungry for the supernatural. Let Your fire fall in the earth. Drench us in Your glory. Raise up men and women who are determined to pray until we see Heaven on Earth. I raise my expectation now for what You are about to do! Thy kingdom come, Thy will be done! Thy kingdom come, Thy will be done! Thy kingdom come, Thy will be done! It is so, in Jesus' name, Amen!

Document Your Thoughts

Day 18

SHARPEN MY SENSES

For false Christs and false prophets will appear and they will provide great signs and wonders, so as to deceive, if possible, even the elect (God's chosen ones).

❧ Matthew 24:24, AMP ☙

Dear friends, do not believe every spirit, but test the spirits to see whether they are from God, because many false prophets have gone out into the world. This is how you can recognize the Spirit of God: Every spirit that acknowledges that Jesus Christ has come in the flesh is from God, but every spirit that does not acknowledge Jesus is not from God. This is the spirit of the antichrist, which you have heard is coming and even now is already in the world.

❧ 1 John 4:1-3, NIV ☙

Discernment is necessary in this hour. Holy Spirit said to me weeks ago, "Sophisticated demons are being released!" These spirits will be in high places, and you won't suspect them due to their craftiness. I want to share a dream that I had earlier this year but let me give some background information first. I gave my life to Christ at the age of seven, and Holy Spirit has been filling me for 21 years. You'll understand why I shared that after reading my dream.

In this dream I was in a shopping mall. I walked down the hall and went into the restroom. While inside I heard a lot of commotion going on in the mall. I walked out of the restroom and back down the hall. There was a crowd gathered in this huge opening by the escalator. The people gathered around two women dressed in clergy attire: black suits with white collars. One woman was a preacher and the other was her adjutant. The preacher was walking around in circles praying in what sounded like "warfare tongues." I mean it sounded like she was really plowing in the spirit. I was trying to figure out what was going on. I wanted to know why this lady was standing in the middle of a shopping mall, speaking in tongues, but Holy Spirit opened my eyes.

To the natural eye it seemed like she was just walking around in circles, engaging in spiritual warfare, but things looked completely different in the Spirit. Through spiritual lenses I was able to see that she was dancing seductively. If you've seen the R. Kelly music video, "Snake," that's exactly how the preacher was dancing. While dancing like a snake, she had her index finger up and was saying to the crowd, "Oh yeah, come on, yeah!" I also saw her walking directly to the people trying to lure them in, instead of her walking in circles. She was seducing and manipulating the crowd, but they had no clue. After Holy Spirit allowed me to discern this, I looked around at the others to see if they saw what I did, but their eyes were stuck on this preacher. If Holy Spirit hadn't opened my eyes I would have never known. Thank God for the gift called discerning of spirits.

Prayer

Holy Spirit, help me to live a life of consecration. It's imperative that I discern properly, and I know fasting and prayer will help with that. I can't focus on surface level stuff. Help me to see past what I see. Open my eyes and ears in the Spirit. Help me to see the spirit working behind certain actions. I don't want to follow someone just because they say the name Jesus. Demons can do that! I refuse to allow a person's ability to tell me my future intoxicate me! Psychics can do that! I really need to become more sensitive in the Spirit, because I don't want to succumb to trickery. I am fully relying on You! I thank You in advance for sharpening my senses, in Jesus' name, Amen!

Document Your Thoughts

Day 19

Demonstrate God

And these signs shall follow them that believe; in my name shall they cast out devils; they shall speak with new tongues; they shall take up serpents; and if they drink any deadly thing, it shall not hurt them; they shall lay hands on the sick, and they shall recover.

Mark 16:17-18

And my message and my preaching were not in persuasive words of wisdom [using clever rhetoric], but [they were delivered] in demonstration of the [Holy] Spirit [operating through me] and of [His] power [stirring the minds of the listeners and persuading them], so that your faith would not rest on the wisdom and rhetoric of men, but on the power of God.

1 Corinthians 2:4-5, AMP

We are living in a time where people need to *see* that God is real. You can quote scriptures all day, but if you can't provide tangible proof, many still won't hear you. There's a lot of talk about Millennials and Generation Z right now. The thing about these two groups is they're going to have to see God's power demonstrated. Most of them have watched their parents and grandparents go to church, pray, and talk about Jesus. The issue is they also saw many of these same people struggle, be consumed by diseases, and die broke! I believe a lot of Millennials and Zers are confused. They want to know why many unsaved people appear to live happier, more successful lives. They've heard all these stories about what God used to do but haven't seen a demonstration of His power. A lot of us want God, but the representation of Him that we've seen isn't very convincing.

I love the revivals of old, but God desires to do something new. He wants to move in a way that the earthly realm hasn't experienced yet. Holy Spirit told me that He is about to reintroduce Himself to the church. It is time to make manifest God's power, not just during a revival, but in your everyday lives.

Prayer

Holy Spirit, help me to walk in power and demonstration. I believe everything in Your word, and I want to help show the world how real You are. People need to know that the God of the Bible isn't a fairytale. They need to see that You still heal the sick and raise the dead. They need to see demons cast out and limbs growing back. Endow me with power and authority from on high. Activate the gifts of the spirit within me for Your glory. I will not fear those who worship idol gods. You answered by fire for Elijah, on Mt. Carmel, and I believe You're going to answer by fire for me. God, show Yourself mighty and show Yourself strong. It is so, in Jesus' name, Amen!

Document Your Thoughts

Day 20

Divine Details

And of the children of Issachar, which were men that had understanding of the times, to know what Israel ought to do; the heads of them were two hundred; and all their brethren were at their commandment.

1 Chronicles 12:32

You may or may not have heard of, "The Issachar Anointing." The sons of Issachar are known for being aware of the times at hand. Those who flow under this anointing can discern the present times and give divine strategies. It is imperative to have an ear to hear what God is saying. It's even more important that you obey what's been heard. Holy Spirit may not release everything up front, but He will order your steps. Many of you can even confirm that God has already been releasing divine details to you. The question is, *will you obey His instructions?*

Prayer

Holy Spirit, help me to discern the times, not just for myself, but for the body of Christ, America, and other nations as You see fit. Download supernatural wisdom into me along with divine strategies. Help me to provide divine insight to those in need of it. So many have questions and You are the God who answers! You're the God of details, and I know You order my steps. Lead me and I promise to follow You. I'm listening!

Document Your Thoughts

Day 21

GIVE THANKS

Now unto Him that is able to do exceeding abundantly above all that we ask or think, according to the power that worketh in us, unto him be glory in the church by Christ Jesus throughout all ages, world without end. Amen

Ephesians 3:20-21

I was in prayer many years ago when Holy Spirit said, "If you praise Me hard enough there are some things you won't have to pray for"! I am fully persuaded that praise pays! You've been praying these past 20 days, but today, YOU PRAISE! Decree the following aloud because the atmosphere, along with the entire trajectory of your life, is about to SHIFT!

Praise

Abba, You're the only wise God!
You're in a class all by Yourself!
Be thou exalted in the Heavens!
Be thou exalted in the Earth!
I join in with the angels, and I cry Holy is the Lord of

hosts!
The earth is filled with Your Glory!
When I look to the north, I see Your Glory!
When I look to the south, I see Your Glory!
When I look to the east, I see Your Glory!
When I look to the west, I see Your Glory!
Thank You for surrounding me with Your Glory: it's my shield!
Thank You for being a God of Your Word!
I'm grateful that Your ways and thoughts are higher than mine!
You're all powerful!
You created the world just by opening Your mouth!
You're the mighty God I serve!
You are the Genius of Genesis through Revelation!
Your ways are past finding out!
Thank You for being the God of war; You always win!
The angels bow down before You!
Heaven and earth adore You!
Even the demons tremble at the name Jesus!
You're the God who brings witches and warlocks to their knees!
You are the Triumphant One!
You're our soon coming King!
Thank You for loving me!
Thank You for never leaving!
While I was yet a sinner You died for me!
You're the mighty God I serve!
Thank You for Your angel armies who work in partnership with me!
Thank You for bringing me through this fast!

Thank You for allowing me to confront my personal issues so that I can be healed!
Thank You for making me free in You!
Thank You for washing me!
Thank You for giving me clean hands and a pure heart!
Thank You for helping me to release those who have offended me!
Thank You for being a good Father!
Thank You for increasing my capacity for You!
Holy Spirit, thank You for filling me afresh!
Thank You for renewing my mind!
Thank You for revealing Yourself to me!
Thank You for teaching me how to live by faith!
Thank You for giving me strength to put myself on Your altar daily!
Thank You for trusting me with Your Word and Your gifts!
Thank You for clothing me with Your righteousness!
Thank You manifesting Your kingdom throughout the earth!
Thank You for sharpening my spiritual senses!
Thank You for demonstrating Your power through me!
Thank You for helping me to discern the times!
Thank You for releasing details and divine strategies!
Thank You for mantling me for manifestation!
Thank You for just being You!
I love You!

Prayer of Salvation

Jesus, I am a sinner. I believe that You came in the flesh and died for my sins. I believe You rose from the grave and ascended back into Heaven. I also believe that You are coming again, and I want to be prepared for Your return. I repent now for all my sins. Please forgive me for all unrighteousness. I want You to be my Lord and Savior. I accept You into my heart right now Jesus, and I believe that I'm saved, by grace, through faith!

Congratulations on taking this step and accepting Jesus Christ as your Lord and Savior! I'm so proud of you! You need to find a Bible based church that can help in your next steps, e.g., discipleship and deliverance. Community and accountability are essential elements in this Christian walk!

Made in the USA
Middletown, DE
24 November 2020